Lerner SPORTS

ROBERTO CLEMENTE

BASEBALL'S BIGGEST HEART

ABBE L. STARR

LERNER PUBLICATIONS ◆ MINNEAPOLIS

SPORTS THRILLS
MEET
RESEARCH SKILLS

Lerner SPORTS
Free Database Trial: lernersports.com

Lerner Publications Company
An imprint of Lerner Publishing Group, Inc.
241 First Avenue North
Minneapolis, MN 55401 USA

For reading levels and more information, look up this title at www.lernerbooks.com.

Main body text set in Myriad Pro Semibold.
Typeface provided by Adobe.

Editor: Lauren Foley
Lerner team: Sue Marquis

Library of Congress Cataloging-in-Publication Data

Names: Starr, Abbe L., author.
Title: Roberto Clemente : baseball's biggest heart / Abbe L. Starr.
Description: Minneapolis, MN : Lerner Publications, [2023] | Series: Epic sports bios. Lerner sports. | Includes bibliographical references and index. | Audience: Ages 7–11 | Audience: Grades 2–3 | Summary: "Outfielder Roberto Clemente of the Pittsburgh Pirates was known as much for his impressive baseball skills as his humanitarianism. Catch an inside glimpse of his life and career" — Provided by publisher.
Identifiers: LCCN 2022011579 (print) | LCCN 2022011580 (ebook) | ISBN 9781728476537 (library binding) | ISBN 9781728478579 (paperback) | ISBN 9781728482583 (ebook)
Subjects: LCSH: Clemente, Roberto, 1934–1972—Juvenile literature. | Baseball players—Puerto Rico—Biography—Juvenile literature. | Outfielders (Baseball)—Puerto Rico—Biography—Juvenile literature. | Philanthropists—Puerto Rico—Biography—Juvenile literature. | Pittsburgh Pirates (Baseball team)—Juvenile literature.
Classification: LCC GV865.C45 S73 2023 (print) | LCC GV865.C45 (ebook) | DDC 796.357092 [B]—dc23

LC record available at https://lccn.loc.gov/2022011579
LC ebook record available at https://lccn.loc.gov/2022011580

Manufactured in the United States of America
1-52234-50674-5/24/2022

TABLE OF CONTENTS

BRINGING HOPE

Roberto Clemente readied his bat at the plate in Game 7 of the 1960 World Series. It was the bottom of the eighth inning. The New York Yankees were leading 7–5. The Pittsburgh Pirates had two outs with runners on second and third base. It was up to Clemente to keep the Pirates alive.

Clemente (*left*) runs to first base during the 1960 World Series.

FACTS AT A GLANCE

Date of birth: August 18, 1934

Position: right fielder

League: Major League Baseball (MLB)

Professional highlights: was a two-time World Series champion; named the 1971 World Series MVP; won 12 straight Gold Glove Awards

Personal highlights: competed in high jump and javelin throw in high school; served in the US Marine Corps Reserves; has an award for sportsmanship and community service named in his honor

Hal Smith (*top*) grinning at his teammates as he reaches home plate

Clemente hit the ball on the ground toward first base. He raced down the line. The runner on third bolted home. Clemente outran the first baseman and was safe. He drove in a run. Pirates fans roared with excitement. The game wasn't over yet!

Next up to bat was Hal Smith. With two runners on base, he clocked a ball over the left-field wall for a three-run homer, giving the Pirates the lead at 9–7. Clemente jumped with excitement as he crossed home plate. Would the Pirates become World Series champions?

In the top of the ninth, the Yankees scored two runs to tie the game. But the Pirates quickly broke the tie with a home run. They had won the 1960 World Series. Clemente's hit was the turning point in the game. He didn't slam a home run, but he brought something very important to his team: hope.

Pirates players and fans celebrate the 1960 World Series win.

A YOUNG ATHLETE

Roberto Clemente Walker was born in Carolina, Puerto Rico, on August 18, 1934. He was the youngest of seven. His father, Melchor Clemente, oversaw workers in a sugarcane plantation. He also made deliveries for a construction company. Roberto's mother, Luisa

Clemente poses with a baseball bat in 1967. He had come a long way from batting with a branch.

Clemente (*left*) hugging his mother, Luisa Walker

Walker, washed laundry for families and helped the sugarcane laborers.

Roberto loved baseball from a young age. His very first bat was a tree branch. He used a coffee bean bag as a glove and tied rags together for a ball.

In high school, Roberto earned money by loading construction trucks and delivering milk. He used the money to help his family. He also bought rubber balls to practice throwing and catching.

Roberto joined a slow-pitch softball team in high school. He busted out long hits and made great catches. He also competed in track and field. He was such a great athlete that coaches thought he could compete in the 1952 Olympics for the high jump and javelin throw.

But Clemente wanted to play baseball. In 1952, he joined the Cangrejeros de Santurce, a professional

FREE BASEBALL!

When Roberto was young, he sometimes hung around the Senadores de San Juan stadium to see the professional baseball players. The players often let Roberto and his friends carry their bags onto the field. This got them into games for free. In 1970, Clemente became the manager of this team.

Clemente in his Cangrejeros uniform in 1952

winter league team in Puerto Rico. Clemente was only 18 and didn't play much his first year. But he played so well his second year that he played in the league's All-Star Game.

SPEEDING TO THE TOP

In the 1953–1954 season, Clemente quickly caught the attention of many major-league teams. The Brooklyn Dodgers, New York Giants, Milwaukee Braves, and other teams all wanted him to play baseball with them. Clemente signed with the Dodgers and began to play for their minor-league team the Montreal Royals.

The Brooklyn Dodgers stadium, Ebbets Field, in the 1940s. The Dodgers were the first MLB team to sign Clemente.

The Montreal Royals were based in Montreal, Canada.

When he started playing in the US, Clemente faced racism and segregation. Segregation is an unfair practice where Black people and white people are separated from one another based on their race. Clemente and other players of color sometimes couldn't eat in the same restaurants or stay in the same hotels as white players.

The experience frustrated Clemente. He thought everyone should be treated the same. He said, "I believe in people. I always respect everyone."

Clemente would continue to speak out against racism. And he continued to play his best. In his first season, he even smashed two game-winning home runs. He looked ready for MLB.

In 1955, Clemente joined the Pittsburgh Pirates. He was one of the fastest players at spring training. He could also throw and hit well. He earned a place as a right fielder on the Pirates and chose jersey number 21.

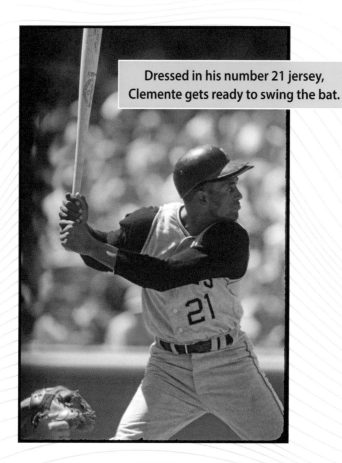

Dressed in his number 21 jersey, Clemente gets ready to swing the bat.

UNBELIEVABLE WIN!

On July 25, 1956, the Pirates played against the Chicago Cubs. It was the bottom of the ninth inning. Chicago led 8–5, but the Pirates loaded the bases. Clemente drove the ball to left-center field. He sped around the diamond and tagged home plate. Clemente had hit an inside-the-park, game-winning grand slam!

That is the number of letters in his full name, Roberto Clemente Walker.

Clemente slugged 121 hits and even scored an inside-the-park home run in his first season with the Pirates. On defense, he studied how balls bounced off the back wall so he could catch long hits quickly and then fire them back to the infield. Pirates fans loved Clemente. Although the Pirates ended the season in last place, Clemente brought hope for a winning future.

A CHAMPION

The Pirates improved with Clemente on their team. They finished the 1958 season with the third-best record in MLB. After the season, Clemente didn't play winter league baseball. Instead, he served in the US Marine Corps Reserves. The Marines helped Clemente

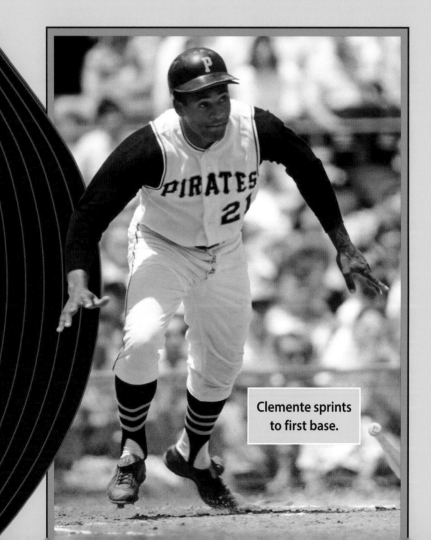

Clemente sprints to first base.

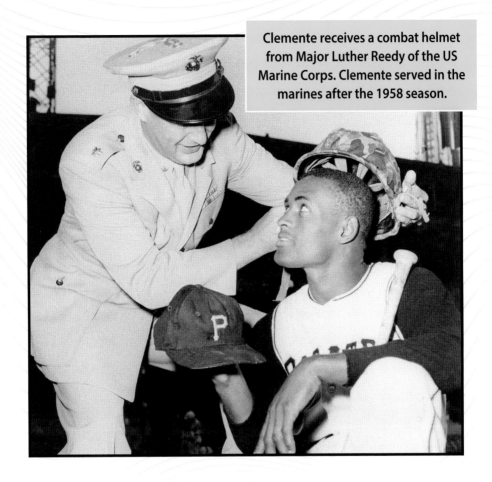

Clemente receives a combat helmet from Major Luther Reedy of the US Marine Corps. Clemente served in the marines after the 1958 season.

gain weight and get stronger. When he returned to the Pirates six months later for the 1959 season, he hit four home runs. One of them is thought to have traveled over 500 feet (152 m)!

Fans celebrated after the Pirates won the World Series in 1960. Baseball fans in Puerto Rico celebrated too. Clemente was popular before his World Series title, but now he was famous. Clemente continued to play in Puerto Rico's winter league. He held free baseball clinics for kids there. And he used his fame and money to help people and fight for equality.

Over the next decade, Clemente won many more awards. He earned the National League (NL) batting title four times, in 1961, 1964, 1965, and 1967. He also won 12 straight Gold Glove Awards from 1961–1972, and the NL MVP award in 1966. He even played in 15 All-Star Games from 1960–1972. Pirates third baseman Pie Traynor once said about Clemente, "He's a four-letter man. He can hit, run, field, and throw."

MAKING HISTORY

Clemente was the first Latin American player to win as a starter in the World Series. And he was the first to earn the NL MVP and World Series MVP titles. In 1973, he became the first Latin American player in the National Baseball Hall of Fame.

Clemente with his wife and their three sons in 1970

In 1964, Clemente married Vera Cristina Zabala. Clemente was still participating in youth baseball clinics, and he soon had children of his own. The couple had three sons: Roberto Jr. in 1965, Luis in 1966, and Enrique in 1969.

Clemente supported older Puerto Rican players too. In 1966, he was a scout for the Pirates and looked for talented Puerto Rican players. He also managed Senadores de San Juan for one season in 1970–1971.

Clemente prepares to swing in a 1971 game.

Clemente was at the top of his game in 1971. That year the Pirates had a chance for another World Series title. Clemente was up to bat in the fourth inning of Game 7 of the 1971 World Series. He belted a high hit. It flew over the fence for a home run, giving Pittsburgh a one-run lead that they held onto for the entire game. The hit secured the World Series championship. Clemente was voted World Series MVP.

Clemente stayed busy in 1972. He held another series of youth baseball clinics and managed a Puerto Rican all-star team. But he had another goal on the diamond too. He wanted to get 3,000 hits.

On September 30, 1972, Clemente smacked a ball to left-center field and cruised to second base with a double. He had done it! The crowd cheered. Clemente tipped his cap to his fans. It was his 3,000th and final career hit to end the season.

Clemente runs the bases after smashing a hit in 1972. He would smack his 3,000th career hit that year.

HONORING A LEGEND

In 1971, Clemente won the Tris Speaker Award for making outstanding contributions to baseball. In his acceptance speech he said, "If you have an opportunity to accomplish something that will make things better for someone coming behind you, and you don't do that, you are wasting your time on this earth."

Clemente warms up before a game. He won an award for his contributions to baseball in 1971.

Volunteers giving out supplies to victims of the earthquake in Nicaragua

When news reached Clemente of a massive earthquake in Nicaragua in 1972, he wanted to help. He raised money for food and medical supplies and planned to bring them to the people there.

On December 31, 1972, Clemente boarded a flight to Nicaragua. The plane took off but immediately had problems. It crashed into the Atlantic Ocean. Clemente, the crew, and the other passengers died. Clemente was 38. Pittsburgh and Puerto Rico mourned the loss of a great player and a generous, big-hearted person.

Clemente had played for the Pirates for 18 years. To honor his life, the Pirates wore the number 21 on the left sleeve of their uniforms for the 1973 season. That year Clemente joined the National Baseball Hall of Fame and received a Congressional Medal of Honor for his efforts to help people. An annual award given to an MLB player for sportsmanship and community service was also renamed the Roberto Clemente Award.

Edgar Martinez (*right*) receiving the 2004 Roberto Clemente Award

Vera Clemente breaking ground for the Roberto Clemente Sports City with her sons

One of Clemente's dreams had been to build a sports center where kids could play baseball, read, and learn life skills. Clemente's wife made his dream come true in 1976 by establishing the Ciudad Deportiva Roberto Clemente, or the Roberto Clemente Sports City, in Puerto Rico. Then she started the Roberto Clemente Foundation in 1993. The foundation carries on Clemente's legacy of love, caring for those in need, and baseball.

Many people still remember Clemente as one of baseball's best. Mark Samels, who helped make a film about

A crowd celebrates a new statue of Clemente at Roberto Clemente Sports City in 1977.

Clemente grins on the baseball field.

Clemente's life, said that Clemente "was much more than an athlete—he channeled that fame into a larger mission of helping people, broke racial barriers and continues to inspire today."

SIGNIFICANT STATS

Won the World Series in 1960 and 1971

Was the 1966 NL MVP

Was the 1971 World Series MVP

Won 12 Gold Glove Awards from 1961–1972

Was an NL All-Star 15 times, in 1960–1967 and 1969–1972

Had the best NL batting average in 1961, 1964, 1965, and 1967

Led the NL in hits in 1964 and 1967

GLOSSARY

contribution: giving or supplying something

double: a hit that allows the batter to reach second base

infield: the area of a baseball field enclosed by the three bases and home plate

minor league: a pro baseball league that is not a major league

MLB: short for Major League Baseball; the baseball league of the highest class in the US

MVP: short for most valuable player

scout: a person who judges the skills of athletes

sportsmanship: fair play, respect for opponents, and good behavior in winning or losing

winter league: a pro baseball league that plays during the winter months

SOURCE NOTES

13 Paul Robert Walker, *Pride of Puerto Rico: The Life of Roberto Clemente* (San Diego: Harcourt Brace Jovanovich, 1988), 56.

18 Bruce Markusen, *Roberto Clemente: The Great One* (New York: Sports Publishing, 2013), 92.

22 "Roberto Clemente Foundation Community Outreach," Roberto Clemente Foundation, accessed February 24, 2022, https://robertoclementefoundation.com/community-outreach-2.

27 Jennifer Robinson, "*American Experience*: Roberto Clemente," KPBS, January 21, 2022, https://www.kpbs.org/news/2022/01/21/american-experience-roberto-clemente.

LEARN MORE

Davidson, B. Keith. *MLB*. New York: Crabtree, 2022.

Denenberg, Dennis, and Lorraine Roscoe. *60 American Heroes Every Kid Should Meet*. Minneapolis: Millbrook Press, 2023.

MLB: Getting to Know Roberto Clemente
https://www.mlb.com/video/getting-to-know-roberto-clemente

MLB: Roberto Clemente Award
https://www.mlb.com/community/roberto-clemente-award

Roberto Clemente Stats
https://www.baseball-reference.com/players/c/clemero01.shtml

Rogers, Amy B. *Positions in Baseball*. New York: PowerKids, 2023.

INDEX

PHOTO ACKNOWLEDGMENTS

Image credits: Hy Peskin/Getty Images, p. 4; Andrey_Popov/Shutterstock, pp. 5, 28; AP Photo, pp. 6, 17, 19, 23, 25, 26; Bettmann/Getty Images, pp. 7, 8, 9, 21; The Sporting News/ Getty Images, p. 11; Science History Images/Alamy Stock Photo, p. 12; Erich Andres/ Alamy Stock Photo, p. 13; Focus On Sport/Getty Images, pp. 14, 16, 20, 22, 27; Rich Pilling/ Stringer/Getty Images, p. 24.

Cover: AP Photo (bottom); AP Photo/Harry Cabluck (top).